WHEN SOMETHING TERRIBLE HAPPENS

CHILDREN CAN LEARN TO COPE WITH GRIEF

written by Marge Heegaard   to be illustrated by children

With special thanks for the suggestions from professionals who work with victims of violent trauma, this book is dedicated to the children who have something happen early in their lives that most people never experience.

WOODLAND PRESS
99 WOODLAND CIRCLE
MINNEAPOLIS, MN 55424
(952) 926-2665

PRINTED IN THE U.S.A.

ADDITIONAL COPIES: For individual
copies send $6.95 plus applicable tax and
$2.50 to cover the cost of handling to
WOODLAND PRESS.
QUANTITY DISCOUNT RATES are
available for hospitals, schools, churches
and others who need more than 12 copies.
Write for details.

FACILITATOR TRAINING WORKSHOPS
are offered in Minneapolis, MN. Contact
Woodland Press for more information.

This book was designed to use the art process to teach children who have witnessed or experienced a traumatic event some basic concepts about trauma and provide an opportunity to learn about and express related feelings. Misconceptions may be revealed, conflicts resolved and self esteem increased while coping skills are developed. The following objectives are included in the text and can be stressed with additional reading from the suggested books. (Check your local school and public library for titles relating to specific trauma.)

I. SUDDEN CHANGE AND LOSS p.1-5
Remember life before crisis
Learn about disaster and trauma
Acknowledge personal trauma
Recognize personal losses

ADDITIONAL READING
Disaster Series, Children's Press
Taste of Blackberries, Doris Smith
The Accident, Carol Carrick

II. GRIEF: A NATURAL REACTION TO LOSS p.6-10
Discover Misconceptions
Discover Feelings of blame
Discuss concepts of criminal justice
Learn concepts of grief

ADDITIONAL READING
Arvy Aardvark Finds Home, Donna O'Toole
What Makes Me Feel This Way, Eda LeShan
Coping With Death & Grief, M. Heegaard

III. LEARNING ABOUT FEELINGS p.11-15
Accept all feelings as O.K.
Recognize and name basic feelings
Identify repressed feelings
Discover feeling & behavior relationship

ADDITIONAL READING
Feelings, Alika
I Have Feelings, Terry Berger
Sometimes I'm Afraid, Joan Prestine

IV. DRAWING OUT DIFFICULT FEELINGS p. 16-20
Identify angry behavior
Learn ways to express difficult feelings
Identify feelings of guilt
Encourage communication of concerns

ADDITIONAL READING
I Was So Mad, Mercer Mayer
Grownups Cry Too, Nancy Hazer
The Colors I Am, Cilla Sheehan

V. SOOTHING PAINFUL MEMORIES p.21-26
Identify fears and guilt feelings
Find power over nightmares
Experience healthy role reversal
Find words for unspeakable events

ADDITIONAL READING
Go Away Bad Dreams, Susan Hill
Scary Night Visitors, Irene & Paul Marcus
Children Facing Grief, Janice Romond

VI. GROWING STRONGER p.27-31
Gain confidence and security
Identify support systems
Recognize personal strengths
Increase self esteem

ADDITIONAL READINGS
Families, Meredith Tax
Your Family, My Family, Joan Drescher
Help, Laura Greene

Reading for professionals: Trauma In The Lives Of Children, Kendall Johnson, Ph.D., Hunter House
for parents: Helping Your Child Handle Stress, Katharine Kersey, Ed.D., Acropolis Books
Self Esteem: A Family Affair, Jeanne Clarke, Harper Collins

ABOUT THIS BOOK

This book was designed for children ages 6-12 who have experienced loss, victimization or family dysfunction caused by natural disaster or human violence. It will give help to almost any overwhelming event that creates anxiety and helplessness that impairs a child's functioning.

Art in crisis intervention can prevent denial, alienation or repressing patterns that occur when children are overwhelmed with feelings they can neither understand or express. Promoting healthy coping skills in children is important because those patterns often continue into adulthood.

Children can learn to recognize and express anger, fear, guilt and other feelings common to trauma. Role reversal and new behavior skills help children develop mastery over repeated dreams and nightmares. They will gain confidence and security as they recognize personal strengths and identify support systems.

This book can be used individually or with a group of children facilitated by someone prepared to understand the specific trauma, accept the feelings and gently encourage verbal communication. It is an opportunity to review the event and discover misconceptions.

Using this book just once weekly for 1-1$^1/_2$ hours is suggested but individual needs may vary. The educational concepts are divided into six units with specific objectives with additional reading suggestions. Each child will need a small box of crayons. Crayons are suggested because they are more effective for expressing feelings than markers which flow easily regardless of pressure.

Invite children to draw the picture that first comes to their mind as they read the words on the page. Do not make suggestions. Trust the child to make decisions about what and when to draw. Children have a natural tendency toward growth, order and integration. Emphasize ideas, children often regress and scribble, erase, cross-out, draw something unrelated or leave the page blank. This is all right. It is the beginning of giving voice to unspeakable thoughts and feelings.

ADULT FAMILY MEMBERS CAN HELP CHILDREN

Take care of yourself and find support to overcome personal fears and anxieties. Children model behavior and coping skills from the adults with whom they live.

Insecurity often leads to hyperactivity and behavioral problems which can be reduced by providing more structure in the child's life.

Avoid any unnecessary changes. Each change adds additional stress. Try to maintain as normal a routine as possible even though this is very difficult.

Explain the crisis and how it will be handled with basic honest facts. Remember that a child's fantasy can often be more traumatic than reality.

Don't force children into situations they fear. Don't ignore their fears or overprotect them with pity making them feel helpless or overdependent.

Share feelings to help children label and name their own. Emphasize that all feelings are normal and O.K. Help children learn healthy ways to express themselves through movement, play, music and art materials. Teach positive ways to express negative feelings.

Encourage communication. Don't assume lack of questions means lack of interest. Be available to observe, listen and talk to detect misconceptions. Expect more separation anxiety fears.

Expect regression and problems. Learn what services are available for your situation and needs through churches, schools, hospitals, community agencies and professional counseling.

Reassure children that nothing they did or didn't do caused the problem. Find time to give additional love and comfort. Encourage extended family and friends to provide comfort.

Locate helpful age appropriate books in the library and bookstores for more information. New situations introduce confusing new words and meanings. This is especially true when law enforcement and criminal justice is involved.

Help children to see police, medical personnel, teachers, counselors, community leaders, clergy, neighbors and other adults as people who care about children.

Age appropriate death education including funerals and burial customs is needed in many situations and is offered in other books listed at the back of this book.

FOR CHILDREN

This is your book. It was written to help you during a difficult time when something terrible happened.

You will learn that terrible things do happen in our world... But there are people around who care and want to help you. You will learn about the many feelings that are part of loss and change.

I think you will find it easier to draw about some things than it is to talk about them. This is your book and you can decide what you want to do and what you don't want to do. Some of the pages may seem difficult to do at first. You may decide to wait awhile to begin, but most children find that big ugly pictures in the mind seem less fearful when they are put on a small piece of paper. You are in charge of your book and your drawing.

No one can tell you what to draw. Draw the picture that comes into your mind as you read the words on each page. Don't worry about how well you can draw or how your pictures look. This is not supposed to be a pretty picture book. Just use colors, lines and shapes to tell a story that is hard to talk about.

Begin at the beginning and do the first five pages and decide if you would like to share your work with an adult who cares about you. You will feel better when you do. Wait awhile before you do the next five pages. It may take a long time to finish this book... But when you do, you will have learned many helpful things.

Sometimes the world is a very wonderful place where good things happen. I remember a happy time... and can draw a picture of it.

Things can change suddenly! Sometimes a terrible thing happens. If something terrible happens in nature, it is called a natural disaster. It could be a flood, tornado, earthquake or

These things don't happen very often.

2.

Other terrible things may happen because of something people do. They <u>may</u> or <u>may</u> <u>not</u> have wanted it to happen.

Something <u>terrible</u> happened in my life...

My life has changed. Some things are different...

The terrible thing happened because...

Sometimes there is no answer to the

6. question, "WHY?".

People may ask many questions. Someone may have acted against the rules of the world and may need to be punished. It can be a very confusing time.

The pain from loss and change is called <u>GRIEF</u>.

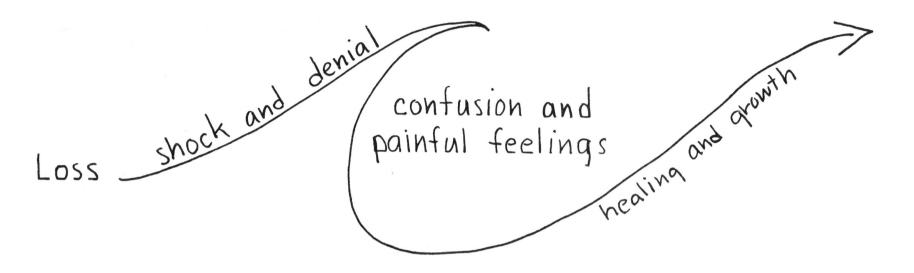

Loss — shock and denial — confusion and painful feelings — healing and growth

Grief comes and goes like waves in the ocean. There will be stormy times ......
There will be calm times...
Grief comes and goes.

When something terrible happens, it may not seem real at first. This is called "shock". Feelings seem frozen and people may act as if nothing has happened... or find it hard to believe something has happened.

Or... people may have <u>strong</u> feelings and do strange things. They may feel and act crazy for awhile!

10. This is normal. It will change.

There will be <u>many</u> <u>kinds</u> of feelings. They
may show on faces.

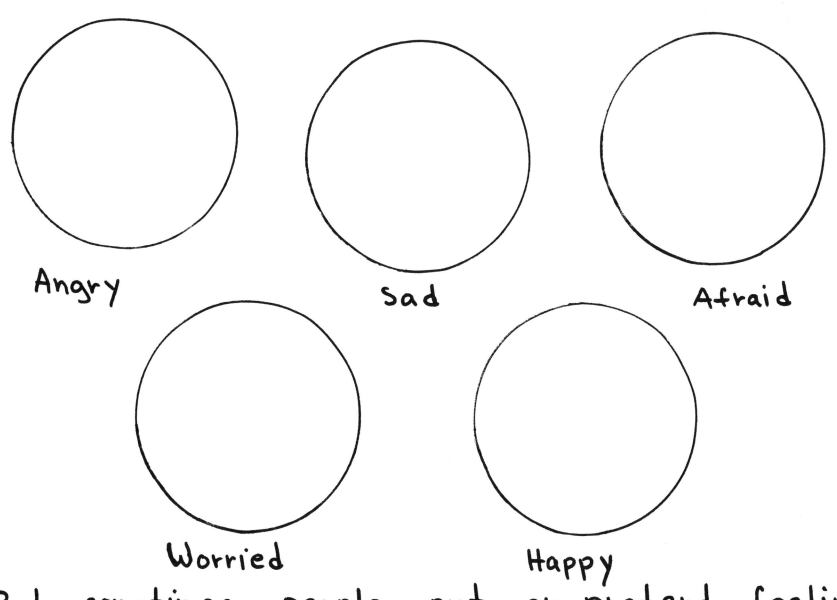

Angry

Sad

Afraid

Worried

Happy

But sometimes people put on <u>pretend</u> feelings
to <u>hide</u> real feelings.

Sometimes people put on a "mask" to hide feelings they don't like to show.
(name and draw 3 feelings you sometimes hide)

with a different feeling

○   ○   ○

_____   _____   _____

Name and draw the "masks" you might use

feeling

○   ○   ○

_____   _____   _____

12.

Feelings are something you <u>feel</u> in your <u>body</u>.

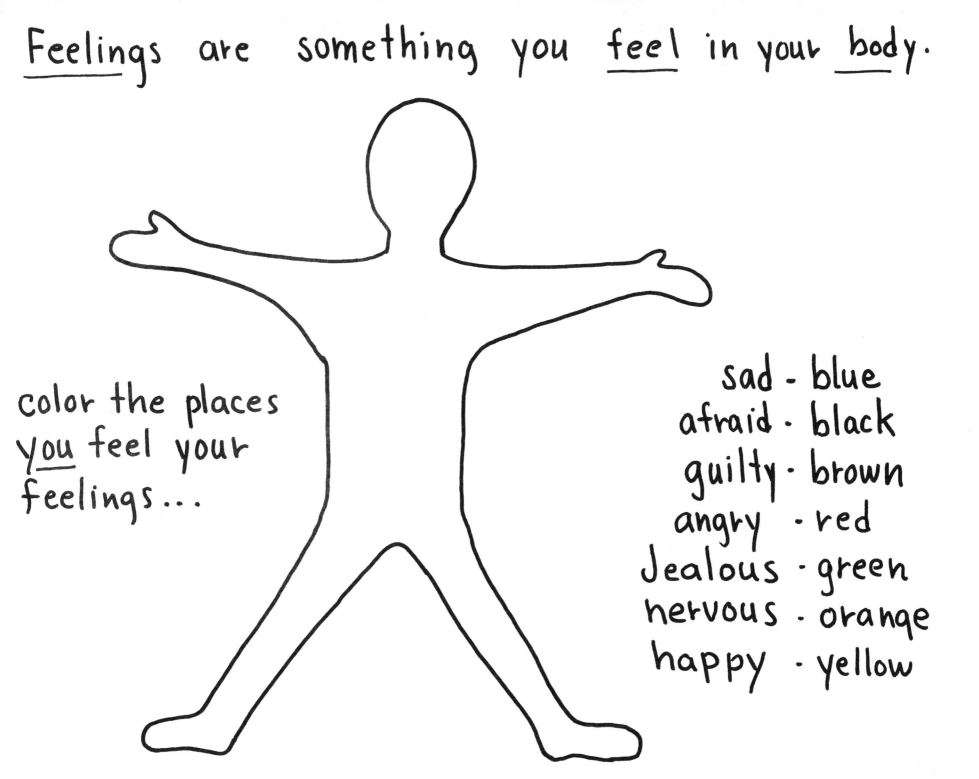

color the places
<u>you</u> feel your
feelings...

sad - blue
afraid - black
guilty - brown
angry - red
Jealous - green
nervous - orange
happy - yellow

13.

If feelings are stuffed inside too long they often cause <u>aches</u> and <u>pains</u>.

<u>Light</u>ly color <u>red</u> where you get little hurts.

Color <u>bright</u> <u>red</u> where you sometimes hurt <u>a lot</u>.

Is this the same place you keep fear or anger?

Exercise, sports, play, music, art, writing and talking are all good ways to let feelings out!

14.

When something terrible happens it may seem that <u>everyone</u> knows about it ... or that <u>no one</u> does!

Almost everyone feels helpless and alone at certain times...

Many people feel angry when something terrible happens. I get angry at...

When I feel angry I....

18.

It is important to let anger out in ways that will <u>not</u> <u>hurt</u> <u>people</u> <u>or</u> <u>things</u>. OK ways are:

1. Saying "I am angry because... "

2. Punching a ball or pillow.

3. Yelling into a pillow or in the shower.

4. Stomping your feet or clapping your hands.

5. Writing an angry letter and tearing it up when you are done.

6. Writing in your journal.

7. Scribbling with a red crayon on an old newspaper (hard!) and scrunch it into a ball to toss at a wall.

8. Walking fast.

Something Sad

It is <u>OK</u> to cry when you feel sad. Crying
lets the sadness out. <u>Everyone</u> cries sometimes.

26.

It may seem that someone or something could have kept this from happening. Who...or what?

No one can change what happened but it helps to talk about it.

21.

"If only..." Is there something you wish you had or hadn't done?

Wishes and thoughts __can't__ make terrible things

22. happen!

I remember where I was and what I was doing when this terrible thing happened... or where I was when I was told about it...

I feel frightened when scary pictures come into my thoughts or dreams.

Awake

Sleeping

(Draw this pictures again on a sheet of paper. Tear it up in small pieces. Throw it away!)

24.

You can change your dreams. Draw your scary dream again... but add <u>someone</u> or <u>something</u> to make you feel safe.

Now... ask the picture what you can learn from it !   25.

It is important to have a place that feels very safe. This can be a real place... or a pretend place to think about.

Some people believe they have a higher power, God, or a guardian angel to watch over them. Do you?

I have people I care about... These people are important to me.

Many people care about me and I will <u>always</u> be taken care of! (List names and write numbers in this "caring circle".)

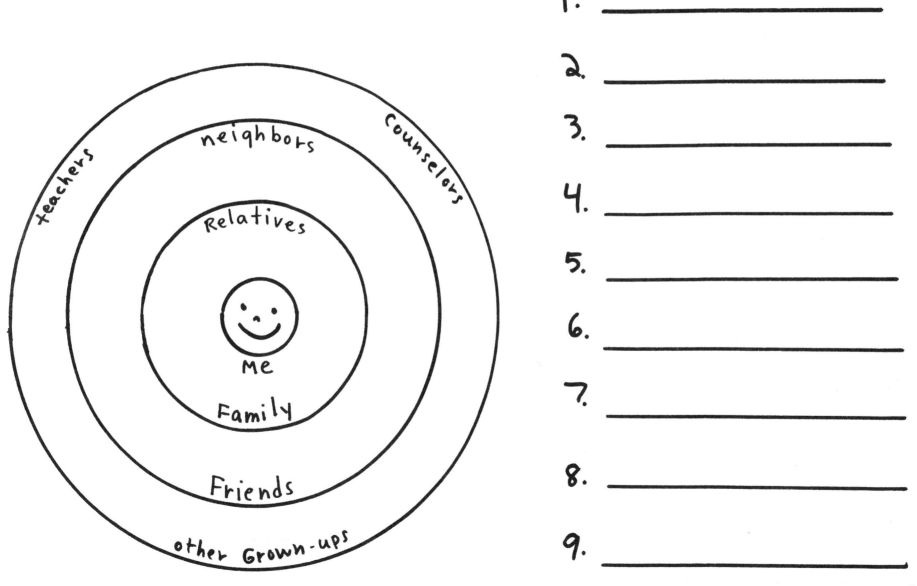

1. _____
2. _____
3. _____
4. _____
5. _____
6. _____
7. _____
8. _____
9. _____

29.

There are things I <u>like</u> about me... (list)

There are things I <u>do well</u>... (list)

There are things others tell me I am good at... (list)

No one is perfect... but <u>everyone</u> is good at <u>something</u>.

30.

Those who live through terrible times will often be able to help others... and someday _may_ do something to make the _world_ a better place!

Even _terrible_ things can teach some _good_ things like understanding, caring, courage and _how to be O.K._ during difficult times!

This is me... I'm O.K.

The world can be a happy place again!

The Drawing Out Feelings Series

This new series designed by Marge Heegaard provides parents and professionals with an organized approach to helping children ages 6-12 cope with feelings resulting from family loss and change.

Designed to be used in an adult/child setting, these workbooks provide age-appropriate educational concepts and questions to help children identify and accept their feelings. Children are given the opportunity to work out their emotions during difficult times while learning to recognize acceptable behavior, and conflicts can be resolved and self-esteem increased while the coping skills for loss and change are being developed.

All four titles are formatted so that children can easily illustrate their answers to the important questions in the text.

When Something Terrible Happens

A workbook to help children deal with their feelings about traumatic events.

Empowers children to explore feelings, and reduces nightmares and post-traumatic stress symptoms. "This healing book...combines story, pictures, information, and art therapy in a way that appeals to children." —Stephanie Frogge, Director of Victim Outreach, M.A.D.D.

Ages 6-12, 36 pp, 11x8 1/2", $6.95
trade paperback, ISBN 0-9620502-3-7

When Mom and Dad Separate

A workbook to help children deal with their feelings about separation/divorce.

This bestselling workbook helps youngsters discuss the basic concepts of marriage and divorce, allowing them to work through all the powerful and confusing feelings resulting from their parents' decision to separate.

Ages 6-12, 36 pp, 11x8 1/2", $6.95
trade paperback, ISBN 0-9620502-2-9

When Someone Has a Very Serious Illness

A workbook to help children deal with their feelings about serious illness.

An excellent resource for helping children learn the basic concepts of illness and various age-appropriate ways of coping with someone else's illness. "...offers children a positive tool for coping with those many changes." —Christine Ternand, M.D., Pediatrician

Ages 6-12, 41 pp, 11 x 8 1/2", $6.95
trade paperback, ISBN 0-9620502-4-5

When Someone Very Special Dies
Children Can Learn to Cope with Grief

A workbook to help children deal with their feelings about death.

Here is a practical format for allowing children to understand the concept of death and develop coping skills for life. Children, with adult supervision, are invited to illustrate and personalize their loss through art. This workbook encourages the child to identify support systems and personal strengths. "I especially appreciate the design of this book...the child becomes an active participant in pictorially and verbally doing something about [their loss]." —Dean J. Hempel, M.D., Child Psychiatrist

Ages 6-12
36 pp, 11 x 8 1/2", $6.95
trade paperback
ISBN 0-9620502-0-2

When a Family Is In Trouble
Children Can Cope With Grief From Drug and Alcohol Addictions

A workbook to help children through the trauma of a parent's chemical dependency problem.

This helpful workbook provides basic information about addictions and encourages healthy coping skills. Children express personal trauma and feelings more easily in pictures than in words, and the pages of this title are perfect to "draw out" those feelings and hurts. There is plenty of room for a child's artwork.

Ages 6-12
36 pp, 11 x 8 1/2", $6.95
trade paperback
ISBN 0-9620502-7-X

When a Parent Marries Again

A workbook to help children deal with their feelings about stepfamilies.

This book helps kids sort through unrealistic expectations, different values, divided loyalties, and family histories. It helps reduce the fear and stress surrounding remarriage and promotes greater family unity.

Ages 6-12, 36 pp, 11 x 8 1/2", $6.95
trade paperback, ISBN 0-9620502-6-1

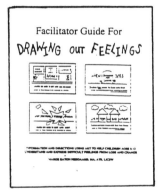

Facilitator Guide For
DRAWING OUT FEELINGS

for
When Someone Very Special Dies
When Something Terrible Happens
When Someone Has a Very Serious Illness
When Mom and Dad Separate

Structure and suggestions for helping children, individually or in groups, cope with feelings from family change. Includes directions for six organized sessions for each of the four workbooks.
99 pp. 8x11 ISBN 0-9620502-5-3
$20.00

SEND THIS INFORMATION TO ORDER

Grades 3-6
64 pages $15.95

Stories about young people's grief and facts about death.

____ Copies COPING WITH DEATH AND GRIEF ($15.95)
____ Copies DRAWING OUT FEELINGS GUIDE ($20.00)
____ Copies WHEN SOMEONE VERY SPECIAL DIES *
____ Copies WHEN SOMEONE HAS A VERY SERIOUS ILLNESS *
____ Copies WHEN SOMETHING TERRIBLE HAPPENS *
____ Copies WHEN MOM AND DAD SEPARATE *
____ Copies WHEN A PARENT MARRIES AGAIN *
____ Copies WHEN A FAMILY IS IN TROUBLE *

* at the following prices:

order amount	each cost
1-11	$ 6.95
12-24	$ 4.50
25-79	$ 4.00
80-(same)	$ 3.50

quantity discounts

Shipping Chart
If your order totals:

Under $10.00	$2.00
$10.01 to $20.00	$3.50
$20.01 to $40.00	$4.50
$40.01 to $80.00	$6.00
$80.01 to $100.00	$7.00
$100.01 to $150.00	$8.00
$150.01 to $200.00	$10.00

Over $200 please add 6% for shipping cost.

FOR <u>FOREIGN ORDERS</u>: PAYMENT IN USA FUNDS ONLY. DOUBLE SHIPPING CHARGES.

Make check payable and send to:
WOODLAND PRESS
99 Woodland Circle
Minneapolis, MN. 55424
(952) 926-2665

Total order	_____
MN. res. 6.5%	_____
Handling	_____
TOTAL COST	_____

NAME _____

ORGANIZATION _____

ADDRESS _____

_____

_____

TELEPHONE (____) _____